Canadian Health Activiti

Encouraging Topic Interest

Help students to develop an understanding and appreciation for different health concepts. Engage students through stories, non-fiction, easy- to- read books, videos, posters, and other resources as a springboard for learning.

Black Line Masters and Graphic Organizers

Encourage students to use the black line masters and graphic organizers to present information, reinforce important concepts and to extend opportunities for learning. The graphic organizers will help students focus on important ideas, or make direct comparisons.

Feeling Face Cards

Use the feelings face cards as a tool to help identify the way students feel during various situations.

Learning Logs

Keeping a learning log is an effective way for students to organize their thoughts and ideas about the health concepts presented. Student learning logs also give the teacher insight on what follow up activities are needed to review and to clarify concepts learned.

Learning logs can include the following kinds of entries:

- Teacher prompts
- Student personal reflections
- Questions that arise
- Connections discovered
- Labeled diagrams and pictures

Rubrics and Checklists

Use the rubrics and checklists in this book to assess student learning.

Table of Contents

halkboard Publishing Inc © 2007   Canadian Health Activities Grades 1-3

My Name Is

My name is _____

1. I am _____ years old.

2. My favourite thing to do is _____

3. My favourite colour is _____ .

4. I am special because _____ .

Chalkboard Publishing Inc © 2007

Canadian Health Activities Grades 1-3

How I Have Changed

	When I was little	Now
1. My size		
2. The food I eat		
3. The toys I like to play with		
4. Where I sleep		

alkboard Publishing Inc © 2007

Canadian Health Activities Grades 1-3

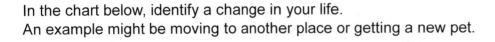

Changes In Your Life

In the chart below, identify a change in your life.
An example might be moving to another place or getting a new pet.

1. **What was a change in your life?**

2. **What happened after the change?**

3. **How did you feel about the change?**

Canadian Health Activities Grades 1-3

A Time Line

	Age	Important Event
1.		
2.		
3.		
4.		
5.		
6.		
7.		
8.		

halkboard Publishing Inc © 2007

Canadian Health Activities Grades 1-3

When I grow Up

1. When I grow up I want to be _____ .

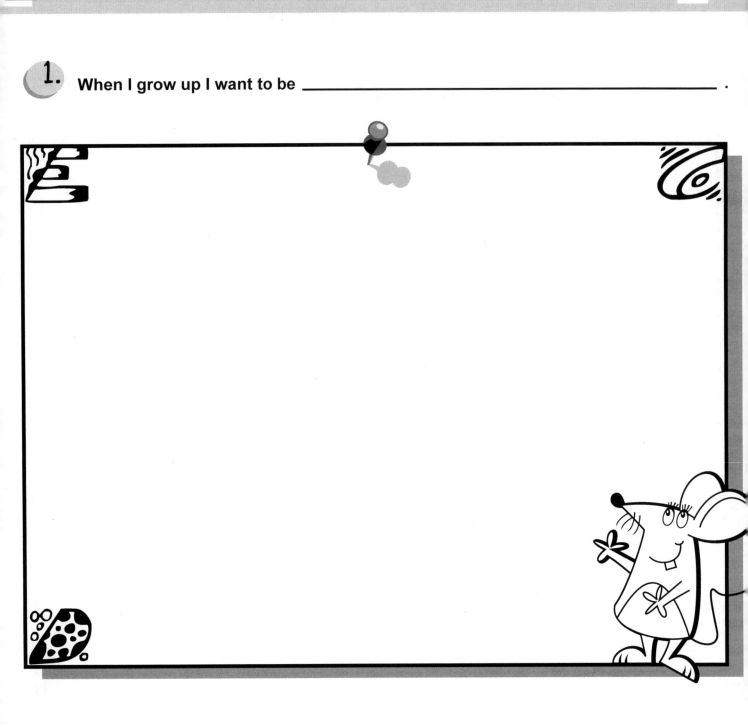

2. The reason is _____

_____

_____

1. This is a picture of someone special in my life.

2. _____ is someone special to me because...

_____

_____

halkboard Publishing Inc © 2007
Canadian Health Activities Grades 1-3

Happy Face

1. This is a picture of a happy face.

Chalkboard Publishing Inc © 2007

Canadian Health Activities Grades 1-3

Sad Face

1. This is a picture of a sad face.

halkboard Publishing Inc © 2007

Canadian Health Activities Grades 1-3

1. This is a picture of a angry face.

Canadian Health Activities Grades 1-3

1. This is a picture of a scared face.

halkboard Publishing Inc © 2007

1. This is a picture of a worried face.

Canadian Health Activities Grades 1-3

How Would You Feel?

happy   sad   angry   worried   scared

	Situation	I would feel...
1.	My friend invited me to their birthday.	
2.	My pet hamster died.	
3.	I am moving to another town.	
4.	I had a good day.	
5.	I had to stay in after school.	
6.	Someone bullied me at school.	
7.	My friend told me a funny joke.	
8.	I had to try something for the first time.	

13

Canadian Health Activities Grades 1-3

My Feelings

1. I feel happy when...

2. I feel sad when...

3. I feel worried when...

Canadian Health Activities Grades 1-3

My Feelings

1. I feel excited when...

2. I feel angry when...

3. I feel scared when...

Canadian Health Activities Grades 1-3

All About Friends

1. What is a friend?_____

_____

2. Name a friend from school._____

3. Draw a picture of something you like to do together.

4. Write about your picture. _____

_____

_____

Chalkboard Publishing Inc © 2007   Canadian Health Activities Grades 1-3

All About Friends

1. Who is your best friend? _____

2. Draw a picture of something you like to do together.

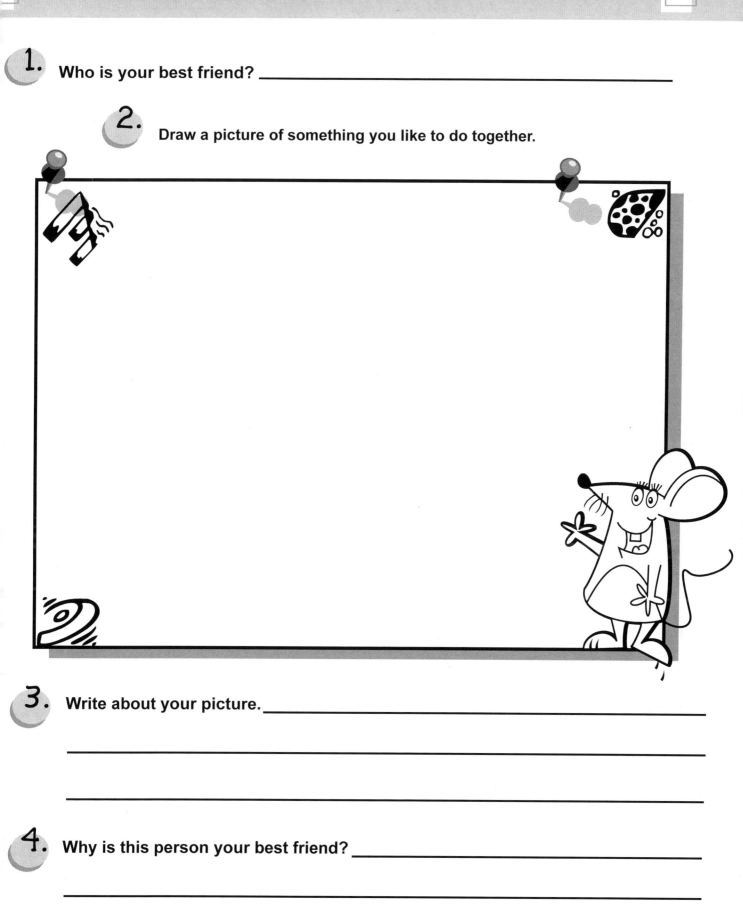

3. Write about your picture. _____

_____

_____

4. Why is this person your best friend? _____

_____

Canadian Health Activities Grades 1-3

How To Be A Friend

1. Pretend there is a new student in class. What would you do to make this new person comfortable in their new class?

_____

_____

_____

_____

2. Draw a picture of something you can do together.

Canadian Health Activities Grades 1-3

Be A Friend T-Shirt

Create a T-shirt with a message that shows a tip on how to be a good friend.

alkboard Publishing Inc © 2007

Canadian Health Activities Grades 1-3

Cooperation Survey

People get along better when they cooperate with each other.
Here are some ways that people can cooperate with each other.
Take the survey and think about how well you cooperate with others.

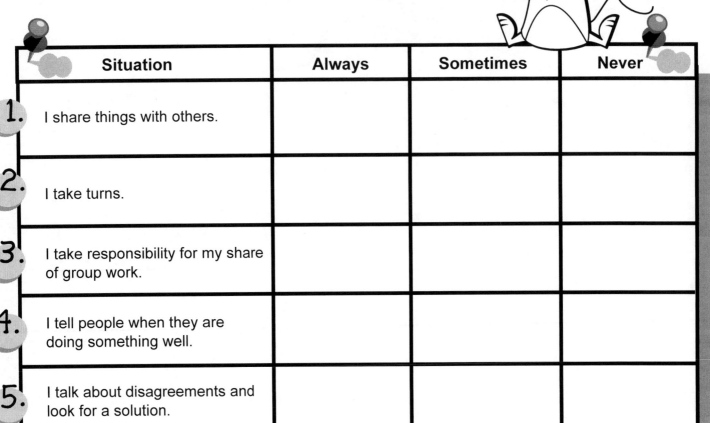

	Situation	Always	Sometimes	Never
1.	I share things with others.			
2.	I take turns.			
3.	I take responsibility for my share of group work.			
4.	I tell people when they are doing something well.			
5.	I talk about disagreements and look for a solution.			

6. **Do you think you are a cooperative person? Explain your thinking.**

_____

_____

_____

_____

_____

Chalkboard Publishing Inc © 2007

Canadian Health Activities Grades 1-3

Likenesses and Differences

Everyone can have likeneses and differences.

Question	YOUR NAME	YOUR PARTNER'S NAME
1. What is your hair colour?		
2. What is your favourite colour?		
3. Who is your teacher?		
4. Do you have a pet?		
5. What is your favourite activity at school?		
6. What month were you born in?		
7. How are your different?		
8. How are you alike?		

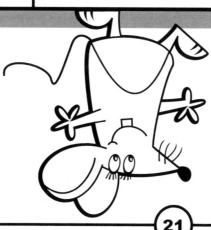

halkboard Publishing Inc © 2007

Canadian Health Activities Grades 1-3

Familiy: Activity Ideas

Activity Idea: What Is a Family?

In a whole group setting, brainstorm with students about what makes up a family. Some families may be traditional nuclear families, extended families, single-parent families, blended families, foster families, or same-sex families. On a web graphic organizer, model how you are in the middle with different family members around you. Explain your relationship to each family member. For example:

- My mother is my family because I am her daughter/son.
- My brother is my family because we share the same parents/father, and/or mother.

The teacher may wish to showcase a different student's family each day. Invite families to send in pictures and to complete questions about their family life and favourite memories.

Activity Idea: Family Tree

Show students how families differ in size and make-up by creating individual family trees.

1. First, model for students how to trace their hand onto green construction paper and how to carefully cut it out.

2. Have students then cut out a hand for each member of their family.

3. Next, have students write a family member name on each hand shape. Each hand shape with a family member name will represent a leaf on their family tree.

4. On a piece of paper have students use brown crayon to draw the trunk of their family tree.

5. Demonstrate for students how to place and glue on their family member leaves onto their tree trunk.

Discussion Starters:

- How are the family trees the same or different?

Activity Idea: Class Graphing Ideas

Show students how people can be similar and/or different by surveying students to create class bar graphs about:

- birthday months
- number of people in a family
- favourite colours
- favourite foods
- number of siblings
- eye or hair colour

Discussion Starters:

- What did you notice?
- What was the most/least common answer?

Chalkboard Publishing Inc © 2007

Canadian Health Activities Grades 1-3

All About My Family

Dear Families,

As part of our health focus on families, please complete the following handouts for your child to share with their classmates. In addition, families are welcome to send in photographs or other special artifacts.

Your participation is greatly appreciated!

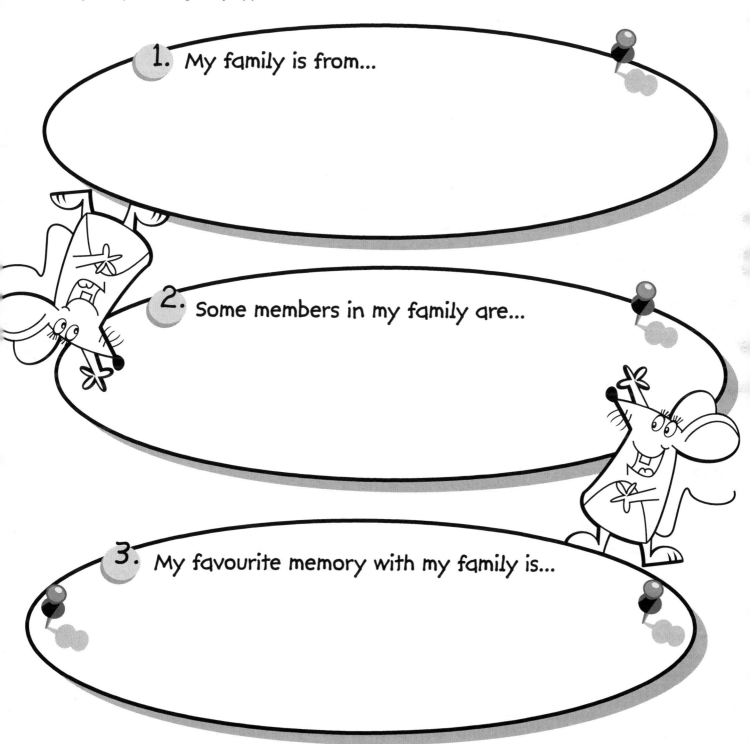

1. My family is from...

2. Some members in my family are...

3. My favourite memory with my family is...

My Family Is Special

1. Draw a picture of your family.

2. My family is special because...

_____

_____

_____

A Family Postcard

Create a family postcard to show and tell about something your family enjoys doing together.

Front of postcard

Back of postcard

To:

Activity Idea: Families Work Together

As a whole group, ask students if they think families are important and to explain their thinking with examples. Then ask children to think about special contributions each family member makes to the family. Record the student responses on a chart. Put checkmarks or tally marks to show repeat answers. Encourage students to think about their own role in their family. What do they contribute? How is it helpful to the family?

Give students a family chart to take home and record how their family works together.

Extensions:

The teacher may wish to talk about how the students and the teacher work together in the classroom.

Activity Idea: Rules and Responsibilities at Home

As a whole group, brainstorm different rules that students have at home. List the different rules on a chart and poll the students if they have each rule at their home. Some of the rules that might be stated are: I have a bedtime, I am not allowed to go near the stove without an adult, I need to be polite, I need to tidy up my toys, etc.

Discussion Starters:

1. Which rules keep you safe at home?

2. Which rules help keep you healthy?

3. Which rules help the members of your family to get along?

4. What do you think would happen if you didn't have any rules at home?

5. What rules would you change? Why?

Activity Idea: Rules and Responsibilities at School

Using paper strips, have the students brainstorm classroom or school rules together. Some rules might include: Walk in the hallways, keep your hands to yourself, be polite, ask permission to go to the bathroom etc.

Discussion Starters:

1. Ask the students which rule they feel is the most important.

2. Who do you think should make up the rules in the classroom or at school? Explain your thinking.

3. Which rules help keep you safe?

4. Which rules help you learn?

5. What are your responsibilities at school?

6. What are the responsibilities of the people who work at your school?

Activity Idea: Rules in Public Places

Do the same as above, but while talking about public places.

Chalkboard Publishing Inc © 2007   Canadian Health Activities Grades 1-3

Family Members Work Together

Please fill out this chart to help your child develop an understanding of how families function and how various family members contribute. For example: sister helps feed the baby, parents cook meals. Encourage your child to think about their own role in your family. What do they contribute? How do they help?

Family Member	Job or Contribution

alkboard Publishing Inc © 2007

1. A rule at _____ is important, because

_____

2. Make a poster about your rule.

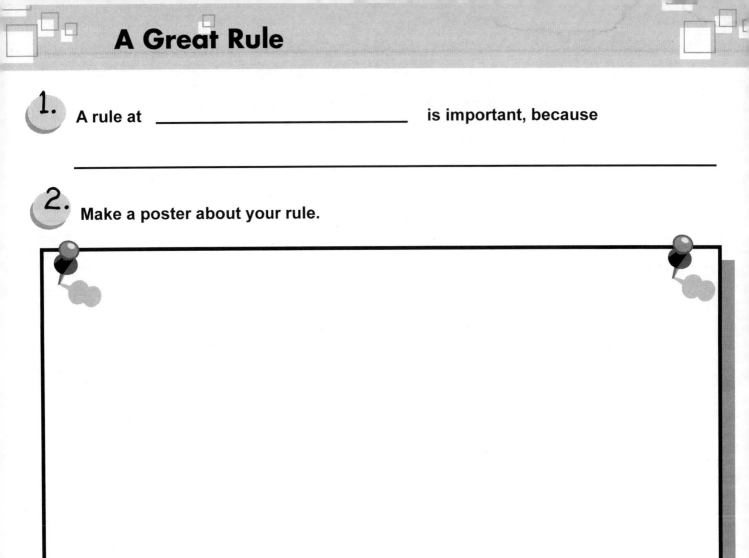

Canadian Health Activities Grades 1-3

Healthy Habits: Activity Ideas

Activity Idea: Living a Healthy Lifestyle

Encourage children to form healthy habits from a young age. In a whole group, introduce the concept of a healthy lifestyle. A healthy lifestyle includes four parts: healthy eating, exercising, sleeping enough and taking time to relax. List the four parts on chart paper and have students brainstorm or list things they can do to support each part.

Extension:

- Invite guest speakers from various organizations to talk to students about how they can live a healthy lifestyle.

Activity Idea: The Four Food Groups

Introduce to students that food can be classified into four food groups. Tell them about Canada's Food Guide and how there are recommended amounts of each food group that kids should eat each day. Different foods give our bodies important nutrients. Carbohydrates like potatoes, bread and cereal give energy. Proteins in meats and vegetables help make our bodies grow strong. Vitamins and minerals in fruit, milk products, and vegetables help our bones, teeth and skin stay healthy. Water helps carry all other nutrients to different areas in the body.

On chart paper post the headings of the four food groups. Have the students brainstorm food items and record them under the appropriate food group heading.

Encourage students to visit the following website and play Nutrition Café. These games offer students the opportunity to test their food knowledge.

http://exhibits.pacsci.org/nutrition/

Activity Idea: Calories Are Units Of Energy

Introduce to students the idea that a calorie is a unit of energy that comes from the food we eat. Some foods like sugary treats have lots of calories. Other foods like celery have very few calories. Reinforce with students that calories aren't bad for you and that your body needs calories for energy. It is only when you eat too many calories and do not burn enough energy through activity that calories can lead to weight gain.

The recommended range of calories for most school-age children is 1,600 to 2,500 per day. Keep in mind that each person's body burns energy or calories at different rates depending on their size and level of physical activity. Consequently, there is not an absolute number of calories that a child should eat.

Extension:

- Would you rather have veggies or a cupcake for a snack? Is that a good food choice? Tell why.
- Would you rather eat some chicken for dinner or a hamburger? Is that a good food choice? Tell why
- Would you rather have a chocolate bar for breakfast or cereal? Is that a good food choice? Tell why.
- Would you rather eat at a fast food restaurant or eat your favourite home cooked meal? Is that a good food choice? Tell why

Activity Idea: Kids Health Website

The following website is an excellent way for students to learn more about healthy habits. There is an abundant amount of information available in kid friendly language. There are also many games and other interactive activities where students can find out about: Dealing with Feelings, Staying Healthy, People Places and Things That Help Me, and Growing Up.

http://kidshealth.org/kid/

alkboard Publishing Inc © 2007

Canadian Health Activities Grades 1-3

The Canadian Food Guide

Grain Products
5 to 12 servings

rice

cereal

bagel

bread

pasta

Vegetables and Fruit
5 to 10 servings

salad

juice

fruits and vegetables

Milk Products
2 to 4 servings

cheese

yogurt

milk

Meat and Alternatives
2 to 3 servings

egg

beans

poultry

meat

fish

peanut butter

30

Plan A Healthy Eating Day!

List the different kinds of foods and portions you would eat in a day.

1.	Breakfast	
2.	Healthy Snack	
3.	Lunch	
4.	Healthy Snack	
5.	Dinner	
6.	What are some healthy drink choices?	

How many portions of each food group did you include on your plan?

Grain Products: ☐☐☐☐☐☐☐   Fruit and Vegetables: ☐☐☐☐☐☐☐

Milk Products: ☐☐☐☐   Meat and Alternatives: ☐☐☐☐☐☐☐

Explain why you think your eating plan is healthy.

_____

_____

alkboard Publishing Inc © 2007

Healthy Or Not Healthy

Cut and paste the pictures into the correct box. Add some of your own ideas.

Healthy Food Choices

Unhealthy Food Choices

apple

donut

salad

milk

banana

carrots

pizza

chocolate bar

Chalkboard Publishing Inc © 2007

Canadian Health Activities Grades 1-3

Healthy Food Collage

Cut and paste pictures of healthy food from flyers and magazines, to create a collage.

1. **Why did you choose some of the foods?**

_____

_____

_____

Canadian Health Activities Grades 1-3

Eat Healthy!

Create a poster with a message to encourage people to eat healthy! Make sure your poster includes a message and a picture

Eat Healthy!

Chalkboard Publishing Inc © 2007

Canadian Health Activities Grades 1-3

Dear Parents and Guardians,

As part of our class focus on Healthy Habits, we would like families to take part in our Eat Healthy Challenge.

The purpose of the Eat Healthy Challenge is to encourage kids to keep a healthy diet.

Challenge your child to have at least five portions of fruits and vegetables a day. Over the next five days, keep track of the number of fruits and vegetables your child eats.

Every time your child eats a fruit or vegetable colour in a box on the chart. At the end of five days complete the reflection sheet about how your child did.

In addition, whole families are welcome to take the challenge!

Your family's participation and support is greatly appreciated!

Kind Regards,

_____

alkboard Publishing Inc © 2007

Recording Chart: Eat Healthy Challenge!

Can you eat at least 5 servings of fruit and vegetables a day for 5 days in a row?
Good luck on the Eat Healthy Challenge!

Day 1	Day 2	Day 3	Day 4	Day 5

1. **How do you think you did? Explain.**

_____

_____

Canadian Health Activities Grades 1-3

Reflection: Eat Healthy Challenge!

1. Do you think you made healthy food choices? Explain your thinking.

_____

_____

2. Who helped to make your food choices?

_____

_____

3. What was the best part about the challenge?

_____

_____

4. What was the hardest part about the challenge?

_____

_____

5. What are your favourite fruits and vegetables?

_____

_____

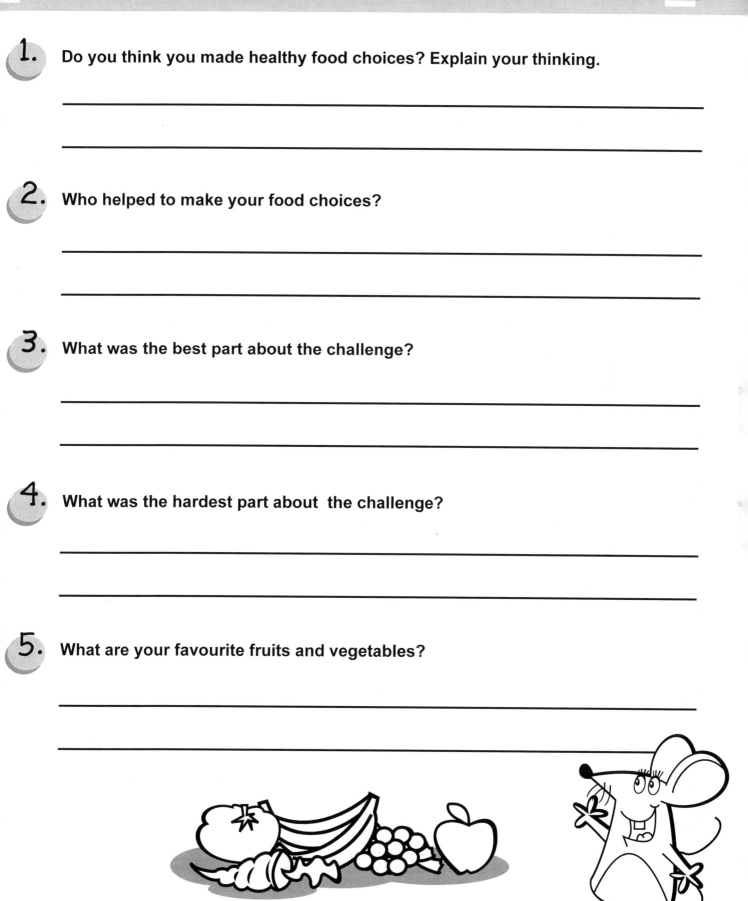

Canadian Health Activities Grades 1-3

How do you feel about completing the challenge? _____

_____

CONGRATULATIONS!

Name: _____

YOU COMPLETED THE EAT HEALTHY CHALLENGE!

Chalkboard Publishing Inc © 2007

Canadian Health Activities Grades 1-3

Healthy Teeth

Keep your teeth healthy and strong!
How many of the following things do you do?

Question	Yes	No
Visit your dentist regularly.	Yes	No
Brush your teeth carefully	Yes	No
Brush your teeth carefully after every meal.	Yes	No
Floss your teeth everyday.	Yes	No
Eat healthy foods	Yes	No

1. **Do you think you take care of your teeth? What could you do better? Explain.**

_____

_____

_____

2. **Do you like visiting the dentist? Why or why not?**

_____

_____

Visit this website to learn more about keeping your teeth healthy and strong:
http://www.adha.org/kidstuff/

alkboard Publishing Inc © 2007

Canadian Health Activities Grades 1-3

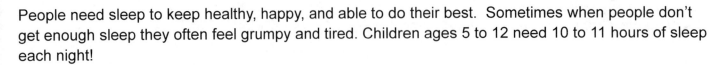

Get Enough Sleep!

People need sleep to keep healthy, happy, and able to do their best. Sometimes when people don't get enough sleep they often feel grumpy and tired. Children ages 5 to 12 need 10 to 11 hours of sleep each night!

Sleep helps your brain, so you can:

- Remember what you learn
- Concentrate and be alert
- Think of new ideas
- Solve problems better

Sleep helps your body, so you can:

- Stay healthy and be able to fight sickness
- Grow strong

Here are some sleep tips for a good night's sleep:

- Make sure you bedroom is cool, dark and quiet
- Exercise during the day
- Keep a regular bedtime
- Don't drink sodas with caffeine

Brain Stretch: Get Enough Sleep!

1. Why is sleep important?

_____

_____

_____

_____

2. How do you feel if you don't get enough sleep? Explain.

_____

_____

_____

_____

Chalkboard Publishing Inc © 2007

Canadian Health Activities Grades 1-3

Create a poster with a message to encourage kids to get enough sleep! Make sure your poster includes a message and a picture.

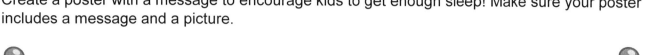

Get Enough Sleep!

Healthy Lifestyle Stamp

Create a stamp to encourage people to have a healthy lifestyle.

1. Write about your stamp: _____

_____

_____

Canadian Health Activities Grades 1-3

People Who Help Keep You Healthy

How do these people help keep you healthy?

1.	Draw a doctor.	**Explain**
		_____
		_____
		_____
		_____

2.	Draw a family member.	**Explain**
		_____
		_____
		_____
		_____

3.	Draw a dentist.	**Explain**
		_____
		_____
		_____
		_____

alkboard Publishing Inc © 2007

Canadian Health Activities Grades 1-3

Healthy Habits Page

Explain why each of the following are healthy habits.

Brushing Your Teeth

Getting A Good Night's Sleep

Getting Exercise

Eating Healthy Foods

Canadian Health Activities Grades 1-3

Personal Safety: Activity Ideas

Activity Idea: Role Playing

Have students work in pairs or in small groups and act out different safety scenarios to show what they would do. Scenarios might include:

- A stranger approaches you, what do you do?
- Your friend wants to play with matches, what do you do?
- You get lost at the shopping centre, what do you do?
- Your friends want you to play a game on the street, what do you do?
- Your house catches on fire, what do you do?

Activity Idea: People Who Keep You Safe

Help students identify people who help keep them safe. These people may include:

- Police Officer   • Fire Fighter   • Block Parents   • Crossing Guard

Invite anyone of the above to come and give a class presentation.

Activity Idea: Safety Tip Poster

Have students create safety posters to promote safety tips for various situations and places. Topics may include personal safety, cyber safety, safety in public places or safety tips for when doing a certain activity like swimming or riding a bicycle. Make sure to go to the website BAM! Body and Mind to find an excellent source of safety information in kid friendly language. Download safety information cards for student use.

http://www.bam.gov/

Activity Idea: Create A Safety Brochure

Have students create a safety brochure. Headings for the brochure could include:

- Who to call in an emergency
- People who help keep you safe
- Public Places: Safety Tips
- Swimming Safety Tips
- Internet Safety Tips

1. Demonstrate for students how to fold a large piece of paper the same way your brochure will be folded.
2. Next, show students how to plan the layout in pencil.

- Write the heading for each section where you would like it to be in the brochure
- Leave room underneath each section to write information
- Also leave room for graphics or pictures

3. Students can then write information to fit the headings. This project could be done as a whole class project, in small groups or individually.

Activity Idea: Journal Topics and Discussion Starters

- What might happen if you play with matches or a lighter?
- Why is it an important rule to only cross the street after looking both ways?
- Why should you wear a seat belt in a car?
- What would you do if there were a fire in your home?
- How do you know you can trust someone? By they way they look? By the job they do?
- What would you do if a stranger approached you and asked you to go into their car?
- Why should you never play with electrical outlets?

alkboard Publishing Inc © 2007   Canadian Health Activities Grades 1-3

Dear Families,

Use this form to make sure your child knows their address and home phone number.

My address is

My phone number is

Canadian Health Activities Grades 1-3

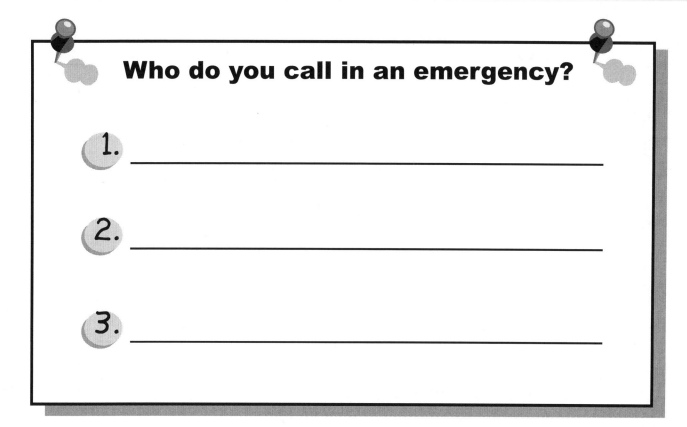

Who do you call in an emergency?

1. _____

2. _____

3. _____

What are some rules you have at home to keep you safe?

_____

_____

_____

911 911 911

911 911

alkboard Publishing Inc © 2007

Canadian Health Activities Grades 1-3

Create a poster giving a tip for staying safe. Make sure to include the safety tip and a sentence to explain its importance.

Staying Safe

Canadian Health Activities Grades 1-3

How do these people help keep you safe?

1. Draw a fire fighter.

Explain

_____

_____

_____

_____

2. Draw a police officer.

Explain

_____

_____

_____

_____

3. Draw a crossing guard.

Explain

_____

_____

_____

_____

alkboard Publishing Inc © 2007

Canadian Health Activities Grades 1-3

Physical Fitness: Activity Ideas

Activity Idea: Physical Fitness Survey

As a class make a list of all of the activities that students might do to be physically active. Answers will vary and might include: skipping rope, bike riding, dance lessons, walks, etc. Once the list is complete, survey students to see what activities they have tried and put tally marks beside the activities.

Discussion Starters:

- What activity is on the list that you would like to try if you haven't?
- How often do you do the activity?
- What do you like about it? How does it make you feel?
- Where do you go to these activities?

Activity Idea: Let's Get Physical!

In a whole group, show students how to feel their pulse. Next, have students do a vigorous physical activity such as jumping jacks, running on the spot, or dancing around the room to upbeat music. Once completing the vigorous physical activity, have students check to see if they feel their heart is beating faster, lungs are working harder and if their bodies feel warm. Explain and reinforce the concept to students that vigorous physical activity is important to keeping your body healthy and strong.

Discussion Starters:

- Ask students to reflect back to the physical activity survey and choose which activities would be labeled as a vigorous physical activity? Encourage students to explain their thinking.
- How did the vigorous activity make you feel?

Activity Idea: Physical Activity Challenge

Encourage students to keep physically active everyday. Ask students to take part in the 5 day Physical Activity Challenge. Each day students will record the physical activities they did along with the length of time. Challenge students to do at least 30 minutes of physical activity a day.

As a whole group, brainstorm a list of physical activities they could do. Some examples are:

- playing tag
- playing sports
- dancing
- skipping rope
- hopscotch
- dance lessons
- aerobics
- swimming
- hiking
- riding a bike
- weight training
- walking/jogging

Other Extension Activities:

- Have students use the word search black line master to create their own word search of physical activities.
- Have students conduct surveys about favourite physical activities.
- Have students create an aerobics routine to an upbeat song. Students can take turns leading the class in aerobics activities.
- Have students write a biography of a sports personality. Make sure students include why they chose that person and what characteristics that person has, to have done so well in their chosen sport.

Chalkboard Publishing Inc © 2007

Canadian Health Activities Grades 1-3

Recording Chart: Physical Activity Challenge

Congratulations for taking part in the Physical Activity Challenge!

For the next five days, keep track of all the kinds of physical activity you do. Make sure you include things like walking to school, dancing, skipping rope, team sports, riding your bike, or playing outside with your friends. Can you do at least 30 minutes of physical activity a day?

	What kind of physical activity did you do?	How many minutes?
Day 1		
Day 2		
Day 3		
Day 4		
Day 5		

alkboard Publishing Inc © 2007

Canadian Health Activities Grades 1-3

Reflection: Physical Activity Challenge

1. How do you think you did?

   _____

   _____

2. What do you enjoy about doing physical activities? Explain.

   _____

   _____

3. What do you not enjoy about physical activities? Explain.

   _____

   _____

4. If you could become an expert in two sports, what would you choose?

   _____

   _____

5. Draw a picture of your favourite physical activity.

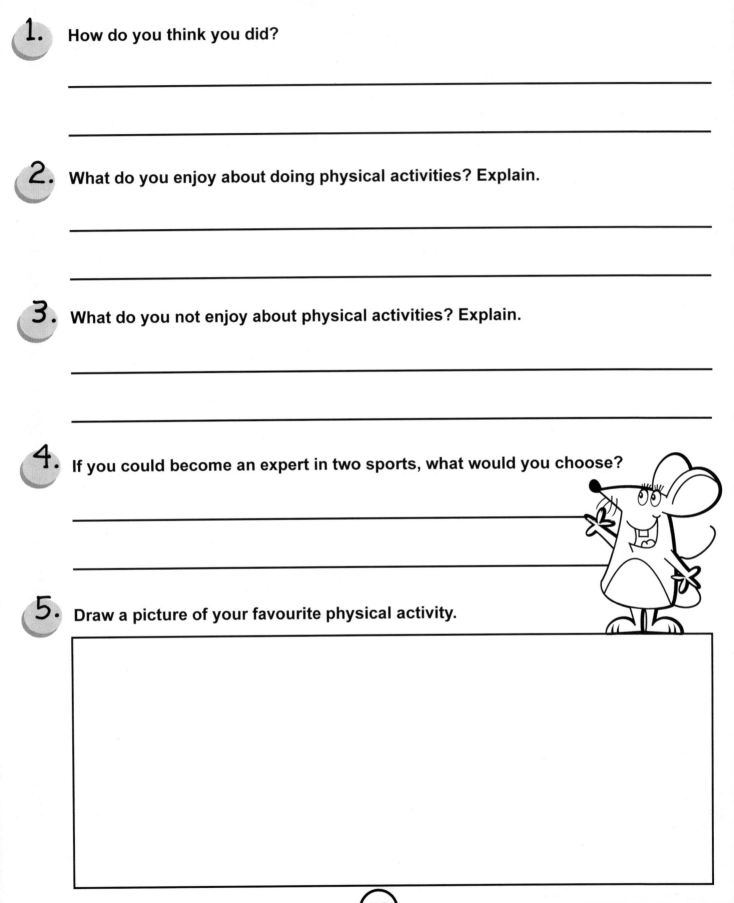

Canadian Health Activities Grades 1-3

CONGRATULATIONS!

Name: _____

YOU HAVE COMPLETED THE PHYSICAL ACTIVITY CHALLENGE

alkboard Publishing Inc © 2007

Recommend two things people can do to have a healthy lifestyle. Make sure to explain your thinking!

I recommend...	Draw a picture.

Canadian Health Activities Grades 1-3

Conflict Resolution: Activity Ideas

Activity Idea: What Is Conflict Resolution?

Introduce the idea of conflict resolution to students. Conflict resolution is a process to help solve problems in a positive way. Each person involved is encouraged to take responsibility for their actions. Clear steps for conflict resolution might include:

- What is the problem?
- Listen without interrupting.
- Talk it out.
- Come up with different solutions.

Discuss and review the above process with students. Role-play different situations so students can practice walking through the process. Students should be encouraged to try to understand the other person's perspective of a conflict. The teacher may wish to use situations that are reflected in their class. Encourage students to come up with different solutions so they get in the habit that if a solution does not work, to try and find another one. In addition, post the steps for conflict resolution on the board for easy student reference.

Activity Idea: When People Feel Angry...

Explain to students that sometimes people can feel angry about a situation. Some reasons people may feel angry include:

- Something is unfair.
- Something has been taken away from us.
- Something was broken.
- Someone was mean or teased us.
- Someone is not sharing.
- Someone is in our space.

Ask students to remember a time when they felt angry. Have students explain what happened and how they handled the situation. Discuss what would be the best way to handle different situations.

Activity Idea: Acts of Kindness

Brainstorm with students what it means to be kind. Record their responses on chart paper. Next go through the student generated list and have students associate the kind of feelings they have around each act of kindness.

Discussion Starters:

- What are some ways you can be kind to others?
- How does it feel to be kind? How does it feel to be mean?

Next, have students create coupons to give out to people as an act of kindness. Coupons could be made for another student , a family member, neighbour, teacher etc.

Activity Idea: Bullying

Help students gain a clear understanding of bullying. Bullying can be described as the act of hurting someone physically or psychologically on purpose. Students should also be made aware that bullies come in all shapes and sizes. Usually someone is bullied repeatedly. Some forms of bullying include:

Physical: hitting, punching, tripping, shoving, stealing belongings, locking someone in or out etc.

Verbal: teasing, putdowns, taunting, making embarrassing remarks etc.

Relational: excluding someone from a group, spreading rumours, ignoring someone, ostracizing someone etc.

It is the hope that if students can understand what a person feels like when bullied, students will develop empathy and help stop bullying.

alkboard Publishing Inc © 2007

Canadian Health Activities Grades 1-3

Conflict Scenario Cards: What Would You Do?

Conflict Scenario Card:

What would you do?

The teacher has told you to line up for recess. Someone in the class pushes their way in front of you instead of going to the end of the line.

Conflict Scenario Card:

What would you do?

Someone in the class has taken your materials without your permission.

Conflict Scenario Card:

What would you do?

You are building a structure using construction materials and someone comes and knocks it down on purpose.

Conflict Scenario Card:

What would you do?

You and your friends are playing with a ball at recess. Another kid comes along and takes the ball away.

Conflict Scenario Card:

What would you do?

You and your and best friend get into an argument. Your best friend does not want to play with you anymore.

Conflict Scenario Card:

What would you do?

You are trying to do your work at your desk and the same person keeps bothering you.

Chalkboard Publishing Inc © 2007   Canadian Health Activities Grades 1-3

Let's Solve The Problem!

kboard Publishing Inc © 2007

Canadian Health Activities Grades 1-3

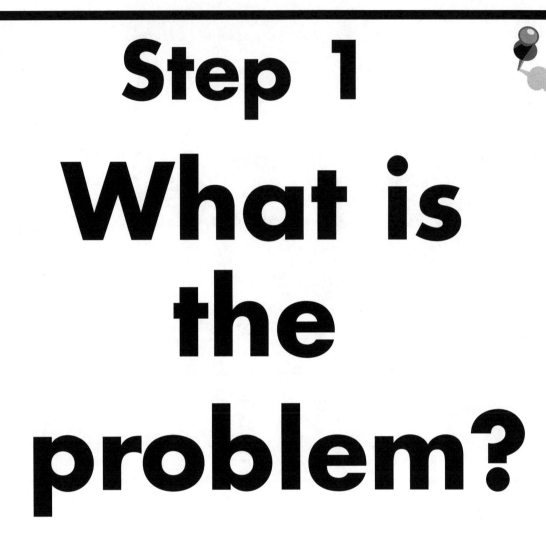

Step 1
What is the problem?

Canadian Health Activities Grades 1-3

Step 2

Listen without interrupting.

lkboard Publishing Inc © 2007

Canadian Health Activities Grades 1-3

Step 3

Talk
it
out.

Canadian Health Activities Grades 1-3

Step 4

Come up with a solution.

Step 5

Remember to put yourself in the other person's shoes.

Acts Of Kindness

Acts of kindness let people know that you care about them. Colour the boxes green that are examples of acts of kindness.

being bossy

sharing your snack

cooperating with others

being rude

being helpful

listening

using manners

including someone in a group

teasing someone

1. How does if feel when someone is kind to you? Explain your thinking.

_____

_____

2. How does it feel when you are kind to someone? Explain your thinking.

_____

_____

Canadian Health Activities Grades 1-3

Bullying: What Should You Do?

1. How do you think a person being bullied feels?

Feeling		Why?
	→	
Feeling	→	Why?
Feeling	→	Why?

2. Circle in **green** the things you should do when bullied.
Circle in **red** the things you should not do when bullied.

ignore him/her

don't tell anyone

fight him/her

go to a safe place

tell a teacher or another adult

stay calm

say you do not like it

alkboard Publishing Inc © 2007

Stop BULLYING!

What is bullying?

Bullying is when someone mistreats someone on purpose like:

- name calling or put downs

- physical violence

- ignoring or excluding

- spreading rumours

1. What are 3 things a person who is being bullied can do?

a. _____

b. _____

c. _____

2. What are 3 things you can do if you see someone else being bullied?

a. _____

b. _____

c. _____

Canadian Health Activities Grades 1-3

Problem Report

a. What happened? _____

_____

b. Has this ever happened to you before?   YES   NO

c. What did you do? _____

_____

d. If this happens again, I should:

- tell the person to stop

- go to a safe place

- tell a teacher

e. Other _____

_____

lkboard Publishing Inc © 2007

Canadian Health Activities Grades 1-3

Stop Bullying! Journal Topics

1. Have you ever been bullied?

2. What could you do if you feel worried about being bullied?

3. Why might someone feel afraid to tell the teacher if they are being bullied?

4. When should you tell a teacher or another adult?

5. Why do people who bully want to keep it a secret?

6. Which type of bullying do you think is the worst? Explain.

7. How do you think someone feels when they are bullied?

8. Have you ever bullied someone? Why did you do it?

9. What can you do if you see bullying happening?

10. Is it o.k. to bully someone because you feel angry?

Chalkboard Publishing Inc © 2007

Canadian Health Activities Grades 1-3

A Letter Of Advice

Choose:

- Write a letter of advice to someone who is being bullied.
- Write a letter of advice to someone who is being a bully.

Dear _____,

_____

_____

_____

_____

_____

_____

_____

_____

_____

_____

_____

_____

Your friend,

_____

alkboard Publishing Inc © 2007

Canadian Health Activities Grades 1-3

Write or draw in the space below.

WHAT I THINK I KNOW...

WHAT I WONDER ABOUT...

Canadian Health Activities Grades 1-3

Reporting Ideas

Non-Fiction Reports

Encourage students to read informational text and to recall what they have read in their own words. Provide a theme related space or table, and subject related materials and artifacts including, books, tapes, posters, and magazines etc.

Have students explore the different sections usually found in a non-fiction book:

1. The Title Page: The book title and the author's name.

2. The Table of Contents: The title of each chapter, what page it starts on and where you can find specific information.

3. The Glossary: The meaning of special words used in the book.

4. The Index: The ABC list of specific topics you can find in the book.

Next, discuss criteria of a good research project. It should include:

- a presentation board or other medium

- proper grammar and punctuation, for example, capitals and periods

- print size that can be read from far away

- neat colouring and detailed drawings

Oral Reports

Encourage students to talk about what they have learned and to make a presentation to the class. Here are tips to discuss with students.

- use your best voice, speak slowly, and make sure your voice is loud so everyone can hear

- look at your audience and try not to sway

- introduce your topic in an interesting way, such as: a riddle, or a question

- choose the most important information to tell

- point to pictures, a model, or diorama, as you present

alkboard Publishing Inc © 2007

Canadian Health Activities Grades 1-3

A Web About...

Fill in the following.

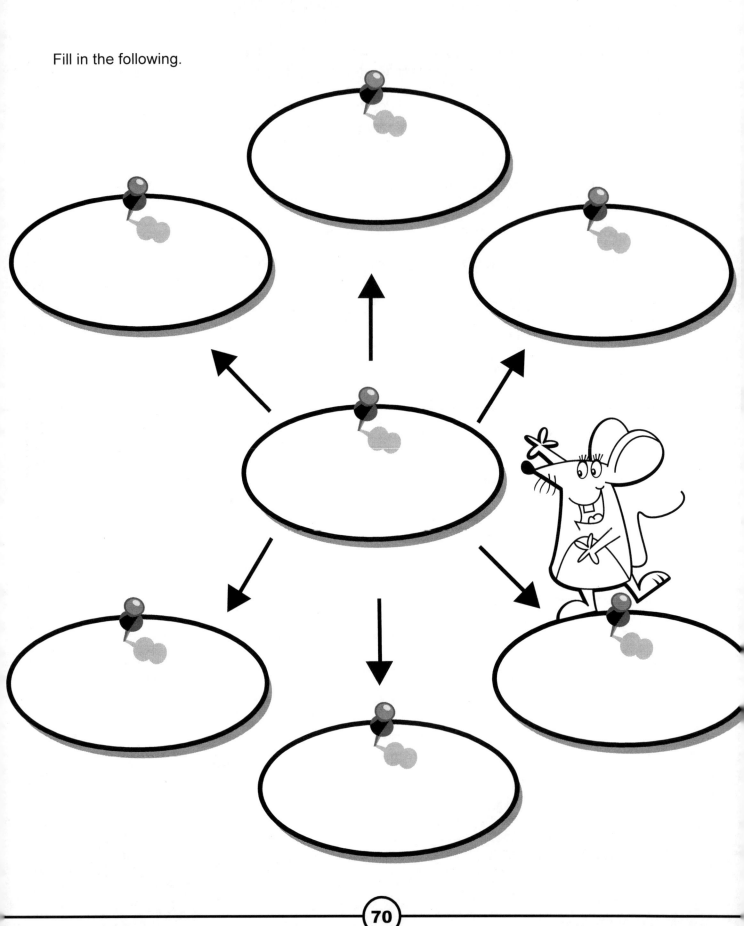

Canadian Health Activities Grades 1-3

A T-Chart About...

Fill in the following.

A T-Chart about _____

A Venn Diagram About...

Fill in the following.

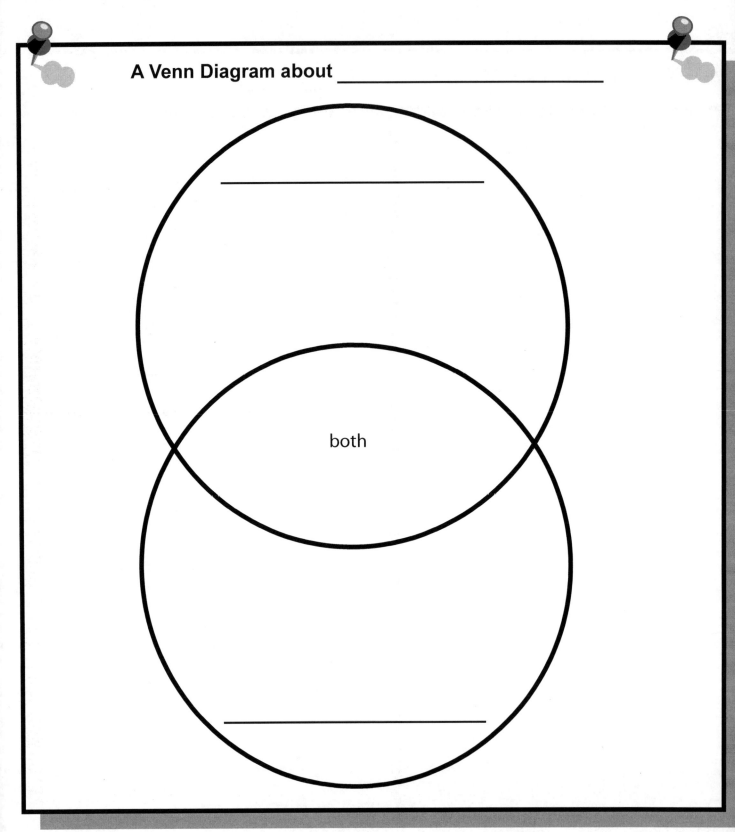

A Venn Diagram about _____

_____

both

_____

Chalkboard Publishing Inc © 2007

Canadian Health Activities Grades 1-3

Survey Outline

1. What is the question? _____

2. How many people are you going to ask? _____

Answer Choices	Tally Marks

3. Once you have completed your survey create a bar graph to show the information.

alkboard Publishing Inc © 2007   Canadian Health Activities Grades 1-3

Conduct A Survey

1. This is a graph about _____

2. Survey Title _____

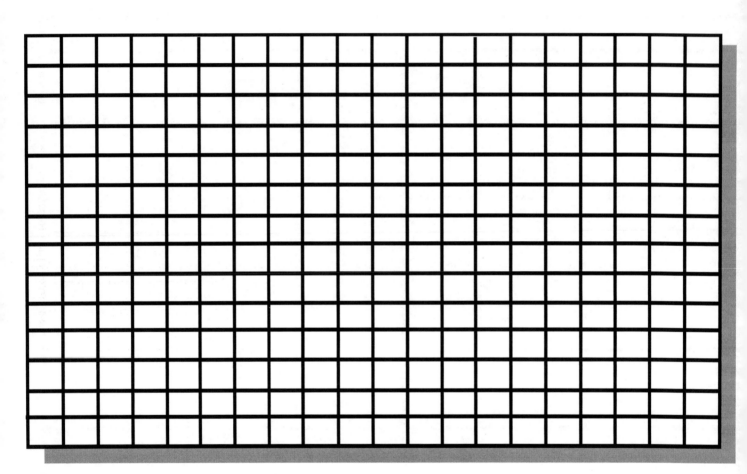

3. I found out that …..

_____

_____

_____

_____

Canadian Health Activities Grades 1-3

Student Rubric

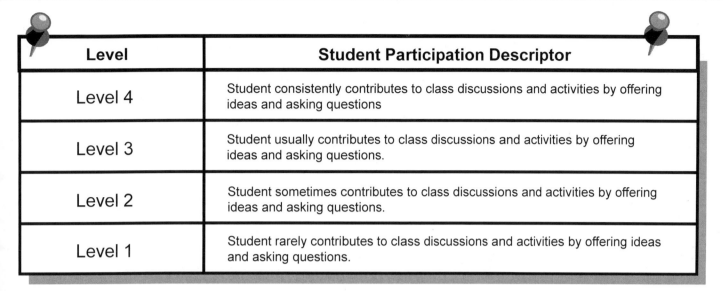

Level	Student Participation Descriptor
Level 4	Student consistently contributes to class discussions and activities by offering ideas and asking questions
Level 3	Student usually contributes to class discussions and activities by offering ideas and asking questions.
Level 2	Student sometimes contributes to class discussions and activities by offering ideas and asking questions.
Level 1	Student rarely contributes to class discussions and activities by offering ideas and asking questions.

Level	Understanding of Concepts Descriptor
Level 4	Student shows a thorough understanding of all or almost all concepts and consistently gives appropriate and complete explanations independently. No teacher support is needed.
Level 3	Student shows a good understanding of most concepts and usually gives complete or nearly complete explanations.Infrequent teacher support is needed.
Level 2	Student shows a satisfactory understanding of most concepts and sometimes gives appropriate, but incomplete explanations.Teacher support is sometimes needed
Level 1	Student shows little of understanding of concepts and rarely gives complete explanations. Intensive teacher support is needed.

Level	Communications of Concepts Descriptor
Level 4	Student consistently communicates with clarity and precision in written and oral work.Student consistently uses appropriate terminology and vocabulary.
Level 3	Student usually communicates with clarity and precision in written and oral work. Student usually uses appropriate terminology and vocabulary.
Level 2	Student sometimes communicates with clarity and precision in written and oral work.Student sometimes uses appropriate terminology and vocabulary.
Level 1	Student rarely communicates with clarity and precision in written and oral work.

alkboard Publishing Inc © 2007   Canadian Health Activities Grades 1-3

Class Evaluation List

Fill in the following.

Student Name	Class Participation	Understanding of Concepts	Communication of Concepts	Overall Evaluation

Chalkboard Publishing Inc © 2007

Canadian Health Activities Grades 1-3

Physical Activity Rubric

	Level 1	Level 2	Level 3	Level 4
Understanding of Physical Activity Concepts	Student demonstrates a limited understanding of concepts.	Student demonstrates a satisfactory understanding of concepts.	Student demonstrates a complete understanding of concepts.	Student demonstrates a thorough understanding of concepts.
Application of Skill Taught	Student applies few of the required skills.	Student applies some of the required skills.	Student applies most of the required skills.	Student applies almost all of the required skills.
Participation	Constant teacher encouragement is needed.	Some teacher encouragement is needed.	Little teacher encouragement is needed.	Student almost always participates without teacher encouragement
Sportsmanship	Student needs encouragement to be a team player.	Student will occasionally share, help and encourage others.	Student will usually share, help and encourage others.	Student acts as a team leader. Student will consistently share, help, and encourage others.
Safety	Student requires constant reminders regarding safety or the safe use of equipment and facilities.	Student requires occasional reminders regarding safety or the safe use of equipment and facilities.	Student requires few reminders regarding safety or the safe use of equipment and facilities.	Student requires almost no reminders regarding safety or the safe use of equipment and facilities.

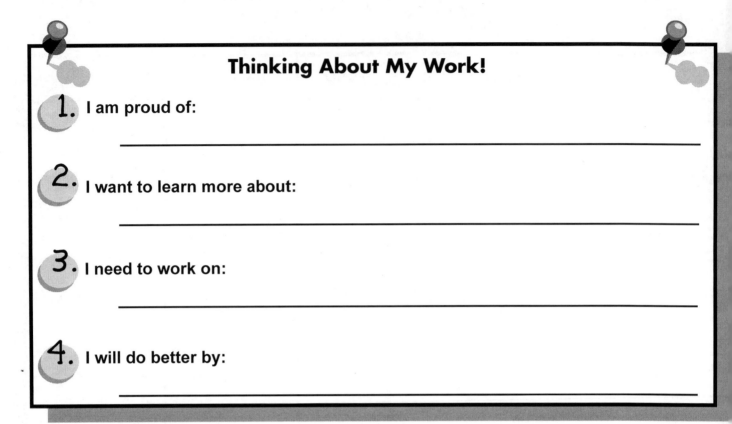

Thinking About My Work!

1. I am proud of:

_____

2. I want to learn more about:

_____

3. I need to work on:

_____

4. I will do better by:

_____

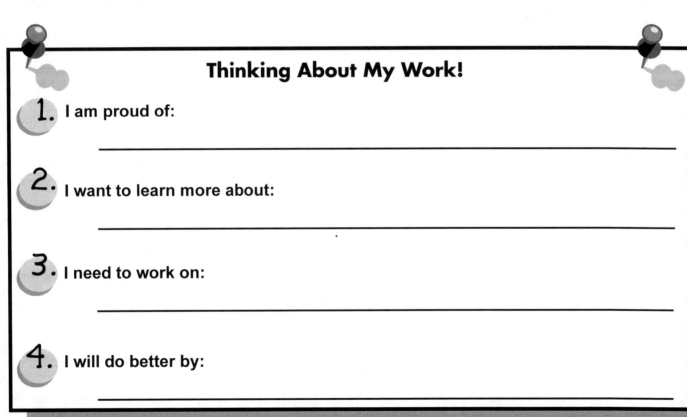

Thinking About My Work!

1. I am proud of:

_____

2. I want to learn more about:

_____

3. I need to work on:

_____

4. I will do better by:

_____

Canadian Health Activities Grades 1-3

Useful Health Websites

1. All About Kids Health
www.kidshealth.org

2. Safe Kids Canada
www.safekids.canada

3. An Anti-Bullying Site
www.bullying.org

4. Stay Alert...Stay Safe
www.sass.ca

5. The Lung Association of Canada
www.lung.ca/children

6. The American Dental Hygenists' Association
www.adha.org/kidstuff

7. Health Canada: A Site For Kids
www.hc-sc.gc.ca/english/for_you/kids.html

8. Canada's Food Guide to Healthy Eating
www.nms.on.ca/elementary/canada.htm

9. Safety Tips
www.cpsc.gov/kids/kidsafety/index.html

10. Fire Safety Tips For KIds
www.kfst.net/

alkboard Publishing Inc © 2007

CONGRATULATIONS!

Name: _____

You are a health expert!

Great work!

Canadian Health Activities Grades 1-3